The Rosary of Our Lady

D0038568

Romano Guardini

The Rosary
of
Our Lady

SOPHIA INSTITUTE PRESS®

Manchester, New Hampshire

The Rosary of Our Lady was published in German under the title *Der Rosenkranz unserer lieben Frau*. In 1994, by arrangement with Scribner, an imprint of Simon & Schuster, Sophia Institute Press published a hardcover edition using P. J. Kenedy & Sons' 1955 English translation by H. von Schuecking. This 1998 paperback edition by Sophia Institute Press is an exact reprint of the 1994 edition.

On the cover: Andrea della Robbia's *Madonna of the Architects*, Museo Nazionale del Bargello, Florence, Italy (photograph © Erich Lessing, courtesy of Art Resource, New York).

Sophia Institute Press®
Box 5284, Manchester, NH 03108
1-800-888-9344
www.sophiainstitute.com

Nihil Obstat: John P. Haran, S.J., *Censor Deputatus*
Imprimatur: John J. Wright, D.D., *Bishop of Worcester*
Worcester, April 4, 1955

Library of Congress Cataloging-in-Publication Data

Guardini, Romano, 1885-1968.
    [Rosenkranz unserer lieben Frau. English]
    The Rosary of Our Lady / Romano Guardini : [translation
        by H. von Schuecking].
            p. cm.
    Translation of: *Der Rosenkranz unserer lieben Frau*.
    ISBN 0-918477-23-9 (hdbk. : alk. paper)
    ISBN 0-918477-78-6 (pbk. : alk. paper)
        1. Rosary. 2. Mysteries of the Rosary. I. Title
BX2163.G8213   1994
242'.74—dc20   94-28899 CIP

04 05 06 07 08 8 7 6 5 4

Table of Contents

Editor's Note:

The biblical references in the following pages are based on the Douay-Rheims edition of the Old and New Testaments.

Preface

The original idea of writing this little book came to me thirty years ago; it stayed with me half a lifetime. I have often tried to carry it out, but I never succeeded, and the plans were put away. This time the task is completed; but even now I do not know if it is a success.

The longer one lives, the more plainly one sees that the simple things are the truly great. But for that very reason, they are also the most difficult to master. The highest task of spiritual writing would be, I dare say, to tell about God so that the heart of man could easily understand. But who can do that? The Rosary is something very simple; and therefore one should speak of it in a simple manner. The reader should feel as if someone took him by the hand and led him into a world filled with tranquil life, a world in which he would meet, serene and benevolent, the holy images of faith. It is beyond my power to do this; so I have substituted my thoughts. May they at least be true and useful.

Part 1

The Form and Meaning of the Rosary Devotion

Chapter 1

Objections and Justification

Oppressive events move through our time and lay a heavy hand on the lives of all of us. Questions regarding our own fate and the destiny of those close to us, and above all, the destiny of humanity, engage our minds and our souls. In religious life the effect is noted in many different ways.

One person may discard prayer entirely because he is surfeited or shaken. He must see that he regains his inner balance; he must try to hear and recognize again the quiet voices next to the loud, to acknowledge that God always remains God, regardless of how powerful earthly influences may be.

With another it is the opposite, and the vicissitudes of life remind him of the Eternal. He feels that things cannot be carried out in a purely worldly way, but must be laid before God, and this is all the more necessary the more decisive they are. So he longs for a place of quiet in which he can meditate and gather strength, to return later to his new tasks with fresh assurance. He needs a prayer that gives him a lingering chance to pause, to collect and strengthen himself. Such a prayer is the Rosary. It has done many a good service. It is this of which we shall speak.

What I write will come into various hands, and first of all into the hands of those to whom the Rosary is familiar. To them I need not explain its justification and meaning, but might simply say what I consider to be important.

But this little book may also reach those who regard the Rosary as something foreign, or others who reject it. For the benefit of these I must clarify certain things right at the start.

Above all, this little book does not try to persuade anybody. The Rosary is a very old devotion which has exercised an immeasurable influence. It is, above all, dear to pious people and belongs to their lives like the work they do and the bread they eat. But when man confronts the restlessness of his intellect and is caught in the whirl of modern life, he loses all relation to the Rosary. Then it has in the beginning no message for him, and it would be foolhardy if someone tried to convince him.

The Rosary is also the subject of misunderstandings and abuses. The Sermon on the Mount says, "But in praying, do not multiply words, as the Gentiles do; for they think that by saying a great deal, they will be heard. So do not be like them; for your Father knows what you need before you ask Him."[1]

The Gospels are the source and summation of all Christian teaching about prayer; one might think that if there is a contradiction to what the Gospel says about multiplying words, it is the Rosary, for it is the very essence of repetition. Also, it is often prayed so hurriedly and externally that one is reminded of the words of the prophet Isaiah: "This people draw near me with their mouth, and with their lips glorify me, but their heart is far from me."[2]

And we must add to this the exaggerations of some of those who recommend the Rosary. At times one has the impression that some who praise it lose all sense of measure when they begin speaking of it.

And then one needs only to hear that there are many similar forms of prayer outside of Christendom — for

[1] Matt. 6:7-8.
[2] Isa. 29:13.

example, in Buddhism — for one's aversion, or at least for one's suspicion, to be aroused.

Certainly all of this must not be treated lightly; but it does not say anything about the substance and value of the Rosary. To start with the latter: prayer is an ancient human act, and contains laws which remain substantial and ever recurring. If in such a serious religion as Buddhism, six hundred years before Christ, we discover a form of prayer resembling the Rosary in certain aspects, it should speak *for* the latter rather than *against* it.

The exaggerations of uninspired eulogists are bad, but they must not darken the view of the thing itself, and even less should one react to them with an equally uninspired rejection. As far as the abuses are concerned, they surely should not be defended. But did an abuse ever mean an actual protest against that which suffered it? Where do we find anything good and noble that is protected against abuses? I fear that whatever is not exposed to abuses has not much value. Man has always mistreated what was important to him, for his love does not have a tender hand.

Should it not make us think deeply, on the other hand, when we remember that the Rosary has been used in Christendom for almost six centuries? Innumerable people have prayed it and loved it. Have they all been chatterboxes and un-Christian? And would one consider such a judgment *Christian* (that is, dictated by justice and reverence toward the religious convictions of our neighbor who also believes in Christ)? If one knows people whose Christian convictions cannot be questioned, and sees how firmly the Rosary has become a part of their lives, one will be very cautious with his judgment.

So in every way, if we meditate on the meaning of the Rosary, we are doing something sensible. He who knows and loves it will gain a deeper understanding; another who saw it in a false light will recognize its true stature; the third will at least have the feeling that he is dealing with something serious, and that to judge it carelessly would be an injustice against both truth and humanity.

Chapter 2

The Chain of Beads and Repetition

We should begin with what is most obvious in the Rosary. An aid is used in this prayer: a string or a chain of beads. Some of these beads are larger or are marked apart from the others by a greater distance. Ten smaller beads follow a larger one and form a *decade*. The whole chain has five such decades. The decades taken together are preceded by a sort of preface, formed by a little crucifix and followed by one large bead and then by three smaller beads.

For the sake of completeness and for those to whom all of this is foreign, we should add that there are some variations of the Rosary that have different divisions, and are only in use in certain places. We should also add that externally the Rosary has taken on manifold and at times beautiful and precious forms, as happens with things that are honored and loved. There can be something very venerable and delicate about an old and nobly designed Rosary that looks as if generations had used it and passed it on.

This string of beads slides through the fingers of the person who prays. At the little cross in the beginning he says the Creed; at every smaller bead, the Hail Mary. At the larger ones that always precede a row of the ordinary beads, he says the Our Father. And after every decade, the doxology: "Glory be to the Father, and to the Son, and to the Holy Spirit; as it was in the beginning, is now, and ever shall be, world without end. Amen." And all begins and ends with the Sign of the Cross.

What does all this mean? Is not this praying cord a symptom of inferior piety, as the critics say? Is it not something material which contradicts Jesus' word of exhortation: "God is spirit, and they who worship Him must worship in spirit and in truth"?[3]

Praying means conversation with God. This conversation is life. But all the expressions of life cannot be reduced to the same pattern. There is no prescription for prayer to be taken "as directed." Revelation tells us who God is and who we are, and in what disposition we should approach Him, but not the precise manner in which to walk and dwell before God. Even words that

[3] John 4:24.

14

deal with spirit and truth do not give us that prescription, let alone the fact that they are often misunderstood; for spirit and truth do not contradict outward form and order. *Spirit* does not mean "thought," but the Holy Spirit who hovered about Christ, assuming at Pentecost the guidance of Christian history; and *truth* is not an incorporeal emotion, but rather the living order in which Christ has placed us before the Father. Even in the seemingly most exterior form of prayer, this order can be maintained, this spirit can hold the reins — just as they may become lost in any form of prayer, even the most spiritual and the most interior.

There is a form of prayer in which man expresses a petition or sentiment to God: an appeal, gratitude, or repentance. This he must do sincerely and concisely, and his expression should be in keeping with his innermost impulse. We are reminded here of Christ's warning against excessive speech. If a person thinks that his request will be more certainly heard if he repeats it ten times, says the Lord, he acts "like the Gentiles."[4] But if in his anxiety he longs for expression, he may well

[4] Matt. 6:7-8.

repeat it ten or a hundred times. Prayer is good when it springs from the heart's impulse; only otherwise is prayer harmful. We mean here all and everything that basically meets God in a false manner. For the "prattle of the Gentiles" is not evil because of the fifth or tenth repetition, but is evil from the beginning, because it is not an appeal to the Lord of creation but to "a god" whom, regardless of his greatness, one harasses like a man to do one's bidding.

But there is another kind of prayer in which it is not a matter of simply saying what is in one's heart, but in which one yearns to dwell in God's presence. This prayer is inclined to use fewer and fewer words, not because it exhausts itself in the saying, but because it is beyond words. Perhaps what it voices is always the same, over and over again. Just think of St. Francis, who spent whole nights crying out, "My God and my all!" At the end even such words will be dropped, and the soul — so claim the spiritual masters — will enter "nothingness." Words in this prayer have only the task of supporting the inner emotion, fading away when they have done this service.

Finally, there is still a third form of prayer. It is also centered around a sojourn with God, around a service to

Him — in inner self-knowledge and tranquillity, but in a manner that makes a flowing channel out of the words in which it is expressed, a force that keeps the prayer moving. In this type of prayer, new words will not always emerge, but the same words will return. Repetition becomes the outer form of prayer for the purpose of pacifying and fulfilling the inner emotion. The Litany is an example of this type of prayer, with its many related invocations and petitions in which the thought is transformed but slowly. It is very old; we find it at the dawn of Christendom. A similar kind of prayer is the use of Psalms, when the antiphon is inserted between the verses — a constantly recurring invocation. The antiphon, too, is as old as the hills. In this form of prayer we also include the Rosary.

One might object that this repetition leads to an exteriorization of prayer. That may happen, of course; but then one has made a mistake and we are using the Rosary in the wrong way. But exteriorization of prayer does not necessarily happen, for repetition can have a real meaning. Is it not an element of all life? What else is the beating of the heart but a repetition? Always the same contraction and expansion — and yet it makes the blood circulate through the body. What else is breathing but a repetition? Always the same in and out — but by breathing we live. And is not our whole being ordered and sustained by change and repetition? Ever anew the sun rises and sets, night follows day; the round of life begins in the spring, rises, reaches its summit, and sinks. What objection can one raise against these repetitions and so many others? They are the order in which growth progresses, the inner kernel develops, and the form is revealed. All life realizes itself in the rhythm of external conditions and internal accomplishment. If this is so everywhere, why should it not also be so in religious devotion?

The Rosary represents a certain form of religious devotion. The individual may claim that he cannot do anything with it; that is his affair. But he must not call this prayer senseless or un-Christian, for then he would show ignorance.

The string of beads obviously has the purpose of diverting the thoughts from certain external distractions of attention. One bead leads the person praying to the next. Their number keeps the repetition within certain bounds, approved by long usage. Otherwise he who prays would have to keep a watch for the "too little" or else fall into the "too much," and thus be diverted from the essential. The beads take this trouble off his shoulders; they do the counting for him. Yet is this not something "technical"? Surely; but does not all life contain "technicalities"?

It is said of all things, even the spiritual, that they have to be learned. But learning requires practice; and practice is nothing else but a training of technical skill, liberating our strength and attention for what is essential. So long as one is yet unskilled, one has to watch every single act, and the essential comes off badly; but with the acquisition and development of technical skill, the essential is liberated. The string of beads has no other meaning.

Chapter 3
The Word

On every bead we say a prayer consisting of words that come from Holy Scripture or from Christian tradition. The word is something very rich, alive, even mysterious: a formation of sounds and consonances by which the speaker gives the listener a glimpse into the inner realm of thought. To a certain degree this might be done by a simple exclamation — an outcry of fright, joy, or affection — although this could not be called a real word. A word comes into existence if the sound expresses not only an emotion or a situation but also an association, a perception, and a reality.

While I speak, the word floats in space, as it were, and what was formerly closed within me is now open. Those who hear the word can grasp its meaning. Then it fades away, and its meaning is inside again, in my own self and in those who understood it.

But with all this something has changed: the meaning became a word and it remains a word. Before it was only the gist of being and life, the inner word that man speaks to himself because he cannot live a spiritual life without living in words. Now it has been spoken, pronounced, and stands open for all time. After speech has died away, its place is no longer in outward audibility, but in the memory of those who heard it. But this memory is a real place in which the word can be found again and examined, and from which it can at all times step into open speech again.

Something else has happened, too: so long as I keep silence, I carry the meaning within myself and am master over it. Even if the other person guesses the meaning, I still have not spoken. But when I speak, I transfer it from my own reserve into the domain of the other. I risk taking it out into the open and thus into danger. Now I cannot extinguish it any more, because what has been said has been said. So speech is the beginning of history — the beginning of that which happens, with all the consequences.

It is said sometimes that the word is spiritual, but that is not true; the word is like man. It has a body like a mortal: the form of notes and sounds. It has spirit, again like man: sense that becomes manifest in the audible. And it has, like man, a heart: the vibration of the soul which fills it. The word is man himself, in his finest and most agile form. That is why the word has such power.

And this is so not only because of the word's outward vibration; if it were only that, the roar of the sea or the sound of a siren would be more mighty. Neither is this because of its emotion, because one might try to detach the emotion from the word — in fact, the manner in which modern man reads today points in that direction. Again, this is so not only because of emotion; in many cases, a mere gesture or a cry expresses much more.

No, the power of the word is explained by the fact that it exists like any mortal, and therefore penetrates into the very essence of life. Who has not come to know the sustaining and comforting effect of a "good word":[5] how its truth engages the mind; how its beauty gladdens the senses; how its sweetness can actually be tasted? But who does not also know how an evil word sinks like a thorn deep into one's soul, so deep that even after years it seems to smart? The word is more than mere communication; it is power, substance, and form.

This is not only true when the word has just been spoken; it is true also when it continues to vibrate in our

---

[5] Prov. 12:25.

memory. The word is not only the self-expression of the person who speaks, but also the assumption that this person can speak at all: it is speech. In the course of time, words and their arrangement have expanded and developed into a world of sense-configurations within which the individual has his roots.

The language a man speaks is the world in which he lives and strives; it belongs to him more essentially than the land and the things he calls his home. This world of speech consists not only of the words that put it together, but also contains sentences filled with meaning: proverbs, for example, thoughts of wise and noble men, songs, or poems. They can confront the individual at any time and exercise their power.

This is true of all words of wisdom, love, and beauty that are retained by man's memory. It is true of religious words that are derived from the experience of pious people; it is particularly true of the words that contain God's Revelation in human terms, namely, the words of Holy Scripture.

Such words express more than mere truth or good counsel. They are a force that stirs up the listener, a room which he may enter, a direction that guides him.

Mary of Egypt was a courtesan in Alexandria, known for her beauty and passion. One day she began to see the light; she went to see a holy man and asked him whether she could be saved. The man of God answered her, "Leave everything behind; go into solitude and constantly say the words: 'Thou who hast created me, have mercy on me!'"

She did as she was told, prayed incessantly, always using the same words. After a number of years, the chronicler tells us, she became as pure as a flame, and the angels carried her to God. Those words were not only a petition or a lesson, but a force; and the woman had such a great heart that she gave it full sway to work her conversion.

The Rosary consists of holy words. The Hail Mary takes precedence over all of them. Its first part is derived from the New Testament. The prayer begins with the message of the angel to Mary in Nazareth: "Hail, full of grace, the Lord is with thee."[6] This greeting is then followed by the words with which Elizabeth greeted Mary when the latter had crossed the mountains to visit

---

[6] Luke 1:28.

her: "Blessed art thou among women, and blessed is the fruit of thy womb."[7]

The second part is an ancient appeal for Mary's intercession. The Lord Himself gave us the Our Father as the perfect model and substance of all Christian prayer. The Creed constitutes the first expression of Christian conviction. The "Glory be to the Father, and to the Son, and to the Holy Spirit" is the glorification of the triune God in its simplest form. Finally, with the Sign of the Cross with which the Rosary begins and ends, "In the name of the Father and of the Son and of the Holy Spirit," Christians from the time of remote antiquity have placed themselves under the name of God and the sign of redemption.

The words of these prayers are recurrent. They create that open, moving world, transfused by energy and regulated by reason, in which the act of prayer takes place. As soon as the person praying utters the words, he has built for himself a home by his speech. The history of his own language and life becomes animated; behind it is the history of his people, interwoven into that of humanity. But when these words are taken from Holy

[7] Luke 1:42.

Scripture, they become an arch in the sacred room of Revelation, in which the truth of the living God is made known to us.

Chapter 4
Mary

Within this room built by the sacred word, the figure of Mary appears as the immediate content of the Rosary prayer.

She has been dear to Christian hearts from the start. Already the disciples of Jesus surrounded her with special love and respect. The reader becomes conscious of this in following the occasional but quite numerous passages in the Gospels and the Acts of the New Testament that speak of her.

The Christian people have always loved Mary with a love especially reserved for her, and it was not a good omen when Christians thought of severing their bond to Mary in order to honor the Son.

Who is Mary? Let us say it as simply as it can possibly be said: she is the woman for whom Jesus Christ, the Son of God and our Redeemer, became the main purpose of life. This fact is as simple and at the same time as far beyond all human understanding as is the mystery of our Lord's Incarnation.

There are two possibilities of greatness. One is to be great oneself: a creator, a hero, a herald, a man of special destiny. The other is to love such a great person; and this possibility seems of equal value. In order to comprehend the life of someone else, one's own heart should measure up to the image of the beloved. What do we mean, then, when we say that Jesus Christ was the substance of Mary's life?

Of course, we have to be on guard. The heart of man, even the most profound, can never bear the same relation to Christ as it has to a loved fellow creature. The limits of the incomparable rise up here, because Christ, though our brother, still has the deepest roots of His being on the side of God. All that was just said about dimension and greatness becomes oblique, and must now be discarded. And yet the fact remains that Mary was His mother. Wherever the Gospel speaks of her, not only does she appear as the one who bore and reared the Savior Child, but she stands living, knowing, and loving in this holiest of spheres.

The lesson of the angel's message alone should suffice for every one of the faithful who reads it aright; it is not the announcement that the divine decree was to be consummated in her, but the question of whether she agreed that it be so. This instant was an abyss before which one's head reels, because here stood Mary in her freedom facing the very first decision on which all of salvation depended. But what does it mean when the question "Will you help the Savior's coming?" coincides with the other question, "Will you become a mother?" What does it mean that she received the Son of God and the Savior; that she carried and bore Him? That she feared for His life and wandered into exile for Him? That He grew up beside her in the tranquillity of the home in Nazareth, then left her on His mission, while she, as the Gospel hints, followed Him with her love, standing, at the end, beneath the Cross? That she knew of the Resurrection and waited after the Ascension in the midst of the Apostles for the descent of the Holy Spirit whose power overshadowed her? That she continued to live on in the care of the Apostle "who was loved by Jesus" and to whom He Himself entrusted her until her Son and Master called her?[8]

Scripture says little about this, but for those who wish to understand, the texts are eloquent; all the more so because it is Mary's own voice we hear. For where else

[8] John 19:26.

should the disciples have learned about the mystery of the Incarnation, about the first happenings of Christ's childhood, and the pilgrimage to Jerusalem? If we do not want to look upon the first chapters of the Gospels as legends (we have to know what we are doing in this case, for we are daring to decide which of the Gospels' words are words of God and setting aside Revelation), we can only say that Mary's recollections, her testimony, her whole life are the foundation of all accounts of Christ's childhood. And they are not only the foundation; for how could she have lived with the Master for thirty years and not spoken about Him after His departure? No one can gauge the effect of her narrative on the understanding of Christ and the spread of Christian teaching.

The course of this life contains nothing fictitious, nothing legendary. It is quite simple, quite real — but with what reality! Legends often sound pious and profound in meaning, often fanciful, and sometimes even foolish. Even when they are really devout, they can do harm. They tell wonderful tales, but often impair and weaken the meaning of something that is much more beautiful and devout, and much more wonderful than all legends — namely, reality.

Mary

The life of Mary, as the Gospel tells it, is as humanly true as it can possibly be, but in this human quality it is filled with a mystery of divine communion and love, the depth of which is unfathomable. The Rosary points in this direction.

Jesus is the substance of Mary's life, just as the child is the lifeblood of its mother, for whom it is the one and all. But, at the same time, He is also her Redeemer, and that another child cannot be for its mother. Speaking of another child and mother in such a manner is like "making conversation": as soon as the speech takes a serious turn, it borders on blasphemy. Not only was Mary's existence as a human mother achieved in her relation to Jesus, but also her redemption. Becoming a mother, she became a Christian. By living with her Child, she lived with the God whose living revelation He is. Growing humanly along with the Child, as do all mothers who really love, releasing Him on the road of life with so much resignation and pain, she ripened in God's divine grace and truth.

For this reason, Mary is not only a great Christian, one among a number of saints, but she is unique. No one is like her, because what happened to her happened to no other human being. Here lies the authentic root of all exaggeration about her. If people cannot be extravagant enough in their praises of Mary, and even say reckless and foolish things, they are still right in one respect: even though the means are faulty, they seek to express a fact, the tremendous depth of which must overwhelm everyone who realizes it. But exaggerations are useless and harmful, because the simpler the word expressing a truth, the more tremendous and at the same time the more deeply realized do the facts become.

It is Mary on whom the Rosary is centered in a focus ever new. This prayer means a lingering in the world of Mary, whose essence was Christ.

In this way, the Rosary is, in its deepest sense, a prayer of Christ. The first part of the Hail Mary ends with His name: "And blessed is the fruit of thy womb, Jesus." After this name follow the so-called *mysteries* (for example, "Whom thou, O Virgin, didst conceive of the Holy Spirit," "Whom thou didst bear with thee to Elizabeth," "Who was born to thee in Bethlehem"). Every decade of the Rosary contains such a mystery.

The whole, as it is expressed in the chain of beads, includes five decades and thus forms a cycle of five mysteries. There are three such cycles. The first is the

Joyful Rosary; its mysteries deal with the sweetly serene and yet overshadowed youth of Jesus. The second, the Sorrowful Rosary, comprises His Passion from the hour of Gethsemane to His death on the Cross. The third, the Glorious Rosary, deals with the glory of His Resurrection and Ascension, the descent of the Holy Spirit, and Mary's fulfillment.

We see how, in this prayer, the figure and life of Jesus occupies the foreground: not as He does in the Stations of the Cross, immediate and in itself, but through Mary, as the tenor of His life is seen and sensed by her, "keeping all these things carefully in her heart."[9]

The essence of the Rosary is a steady incitement to holy sympathy. If a person becomes very important to us, we are happy to meet someone who is attached to him. We see his image mirrored in another life and we see it anew. Our eyes meet two eyes that also love and see. Those eyes add their range of vision to ours, and our gaze may now go beyond the narrowness of our own ego and embrace the beloved being, previously seen only from one side. The joys that the other person experienced, and also the pains he suffered, become so many strings

[9] Luke 2:51.

whose vibrations draw from our heart new notes, new understanding, and new responses.

It is intrinsic in the virtue of sympathy that the other person puts his life at our disposal, which enables us to see and to love not only with our own senses but also with his. Something of this sort, only on a higher plane, happens with the Rosary.

Chapter 5

Christ in Us

To linger in the domain of Mary is a divinely great thing. One does not ask about the utility of truly noble things, because they have their meaning within themselves. So it is of infinite meaning to draw a deep breath of this purity, to be secure in the peace of this union with God.

With this we come back to what we said in the beginning. Man needs a place of holy tranquillity that the breath of God pervades and where he meets the great figures of the Faith. This place is the inaccessibility of God Himself, which only Christ opens to man.

All prayer begins by man becoming silent — recollecting his scattered thoughts, feeling remorse at his trespasses, and directing his thoughts toward God. If man does all this, this place is thrown open, not only as a domain of spiritual tranquillity and mental concentration, but as something that comes from God.

We are always in need of this place, especially when the convulsions of the times make clear something that has always existed but which is sometimes hidden by outward well-being and a prevailing peace of mind: namely, the homelessness of our lives. In such times, a great courage is demanded from us: not only a readiness to dispense with more and to accomplish more than usual, but to persevere in a vacuum we do not otherwise notice. So we require more than ever this place of which we speak, not to creep into as a hiding place, but as a place to find the core of things, to become calm and confident once more.

For this reason the Rosary is so important in times like ours — assuming, of course, that all slackness and exaggeration are done away with, and that it is used in its clear and original forcefulness. This is all the more important because the Rosary does not require any special preparation, and the petitioner does not need to generate thoughts of which he is not capable at the moment or at any other time. Rather, he steps into a well-ordered world, meets familiar images, and finds roads that lead him to the essential.

The Rosary has the character of a sojourn. Its essence is the sheltering security of a quiet, holy world that envelops the person who is praying. This is particularly evident when we compare it with the Stations of the

Cross, which have the character of a journey. The worshipper follows the Master from one station to another, and feels at the end that he has reached his goal. The Rosary is not a road, but a place, and it has no goal but a depth. To linger in it has great compensations.

Into this place the worshipper may carry all his petitions. The second part of the Hail Mary is a request, and he may fill it with his fondest wishes. The Mother of our Lord is not a goddess who lives far above men in all her splendor and has no care for them. What happened to her happened for humanity's sake. He who was her Child is our Redeemer. She is one of us, even if she met our common destiny in a way that is her very own.

The Christian heart has always known Mary as the essence of compassion and love, to whom men can turn with particular and unreserved confidence. This is expressed so well by the intimate name that was given her from the beginning: the name of *mother*. When Christian hearts begin to beat, they know that Mary is theirs because she is the mother of Christ. The same maternal mystery in her surrounds Christ, "the firstborn among many brethren,"[10] and us. Christians have at all times

[10] Rom. 8:29.

carried their petitions to Mary with the conviction that they were doing right.

There is something stupendous in the profusion of human petitions that find expression in the Hail Mary: that she may intercede for us "now and at the hour of our death." There is no naming of details. Every human need is included, and we all employ the same words to portray our misery.

Only at two instants can we grasp this human need, instants that are decisive in our lives. The one is the "now," the hour in which we have to fulfill the will of God, to choose between good and evil, and so decide the course of our eternal destiny. The other one is "the hour of our death," which terminates our life, giving to all deeds and past happenings the character that will count for them in eternity.

To this we must add something else. To say the Rosary correctly is not easy, and I must ask the reader not to dwell on single words but to strive to find their right meaning.

The Apostle Paul speaks in his letters again and again of an ultimate mystery of Christian existence: namely, that Christ dwells "in us." "It is now no longer

I that live, but Christ lives in me," he says in his message to the Galatians.[11] He exhorts us to be faithful and vigilant, "until Christ is formed in you."[12] He sees the significance of Christian growth in "the deep knowledge of the Son of God, to perfect manhood, to the mature measure of the fullness of Christ,"[13] and in "becoming conformed to the image of His Son, that He should be the firstborn among many brethren."[14]

This, in the first place, is an expression of the unity of faith and the communion of grace, just as one may say of a person that a venerated model lives in him. But there is more significance to this, more from a human standpoint: namely, a communion that surpasses the joint indwelling of grace and mercy, of conviction and loyal allegiance; a participation in the reality of Christ that cannot be felt deeply enough. There is more significance also in the eyes of God; and we only rightly value the meaning of these words if we seek to understand what they mean to God.

[11] Gal. 2:20.
[12] Gal. 4:19.
[13] Eph. 4:13.
[14] Rom. 8:29.

God loves man. We say and hear this again and again. But it seems that this message is not always understood in its whole gravity. For it means not only that God is kindly disposed to man, that He pardons his sins, gives him the strength to lead a virtuous life, and leads him toward that likeness to God which is the meaning of creation. Surely all of this must not be treated with disdain. It should be enough and more than enough, and, anyway, it would be senseless in this case to lay such things on a scale. But we see that it is not enough when we use the measurements that God Himself has placed in our hands: namely, what He has done for His love's sake.

God has taken the task of atoning for our sins upon Himself; in the human nature which He assumed, He became man, remained man, and keeps the human form eternally. He has lived among us, accepted the death that was decreed for Him, and made of it an atonement for our sins. We must put an end to the attitude of taking it for granted when we hear and accept all this. As a matter of fact, it is something tremendous, indeed even irrational, if one measures it by what man of himself can understand about God and even about humans. From our standpoint, we must say that this is by rights "not becoming to God." Here obviously is more than mere benevolent love, a pure and mighty act of graciousness. Here must be found a motive in action that concerns God Himself, and we can only express it by saying that His love must have meant *fate* for Him from the beginning. The word is uncommon, but I do not find a better one; so I must ask the reader to try and understand what is meant by it.

To say that God's love meant *fate* for Him certainly means nothing that would diminish God's honor, but on the contrary, something that should teach us to adore Him all the more deeply. A person who loves relinquishes the freedom of the untouched heart, and becomes chained to the beloved, not by force or necessity but precisely by love. He cannot say of the other any more, "This is someone else, not I — this hits him, not me!" Such distinctions disappear with the degree of love's reality.

Therefore, love is fate from the first moment. Something similar must be true with God. Again, this is not said correctly, for what happens to the loving individual must be only a reflection of what happens in God with unbelievable import and power. One might object that such thoughts might encroach upon God's freedom, and that He, who is Lord of all, might be brought into a position of dependency. If that happened, such thoughts would surely be false, for the foundation and guarantee of our salvation is the truth that God is the Master; He is independent, self-sufficient, and almighty.

And yet this same God has loved man from the start, and loved him in divine truth. So man's commissions and omissions are not consummated "beneath" God, so to speak, and pursued by Him with the eyes of affection but still as something that does not concern Him. Loving man, God has in a way allowed man's fate to touch His heart. He has united His honor — the honor of a loving Creator — with the salvation of His creature in such a manner that whatever happens to this creature becomes His own fate.

Again, one might object that no creature by virtue of his own power can have any significance in the eyes of God, least of all man who sins and becomes God's contradiction. One might object that God's love can find no worthy object, being a consummate motive in itself. That is very true! No creature can, of his own power, draw down God's love upon himself, because the creature has nothing to offer of his own. Whatever he has and is, he has from God. But he has it very truly from

Him — and that establishes its validity before Him. Otherwise, what could it mean that God Himself, looking at His work of creation, declared with mounting emphasis that all He had made was "good." It was indeed "good"; in fact, it was "very good" in His eyes.[15]

Here begins the self-investment of the honor of a loving Creator of which we spoke before. It continues when it is said of man that he was created in God's image, for this means that God has placed the honor of His own image into man; and as His motive was love, it further means that He is now united with this man in a manner that cannot be compared to a loving union on the human plane. This self-investment grows deeper and more inexorable with the advent of God into the course of sacred history, with the covenant He formed with man, and with the revelation of His holy truth and decrees — up to the event of the Incarnation, a deed that burst asunder all and every earthly scale.

To be of real importance to Him is a gift God gave to man. It is the beginning of His love. There must be a mysterious longing for man in God. In the eyes of the infinite Eternal, in the eyes of the Lord who is and

[15] Gen. 1:4, 31.

possesses all, man must be very precious, and God wants to have a share of him.

This is the mystery to which the spiritual masters refer when they speak of God's birth in man. God not only strives to be man's helper and guardian, as He is with all that has being, but to have a share in his existence, to enter it, transfer Himself into it, to become the Son of Man. This happened, once and for all, in the Incarnation of the Son of God. Christ's life is the essential and substantial fulfillment of God's love expressed to man. In Christ, God has presented Himself to man; but in Christ He has also claimed His share of him.

God took upon Himself human form; thus he who sees Jesus sees God.[16] This means that he has not only the grace to recognize God in Jesus, but also God's joy at dwelling as a human being in Christ. What has happened in Christ, once and for all, shall be consummated over and over again, says St. Paul. Not that it will happen again physically — the Incarnation is a divinely personal event of indisputable uniqueness — but spiritually, so that it can be re-enacted in every individual man. Yes, really, in every one.

[16] John 14:9.

No one is dispensable, for every one exists only once, and God loves man so much that He wants to renew the mystery of the Incarnation in every one of us. To become a true believer means to receive the risen Christ within us. To live the life of faith is to make room for Him, so that He may express Himself and grow within oneself.

Faith is finally fulfilled when Christ penetrates a man's being and becomes his one and all. The life of Christ is the theme that is given and carried out in every man anew. More and more Christ enters into his life, and God in Christ; evermore man's human side is led across to Christ, and through Christ to God.

In this manner the new man is created,[17] in whom the Lord lives again, in whom God sates His love. Through this, man becomes what God wants him to be. The Rosary conforms to this mystery. What happened in Mary does not concern us at a holy distance, but fashions for us the unique, unattainable, and yet primal form of what should take place in the life of every Christian: the "taking shape" of the eternal Son of God in the life of the man of faith.

[17] Eph. 4:24.

The Rosary of Our Lady

When that man meets the figures that make up the cast of the Rosary, he comes close to the primal form of this proceeding, and the hidden spark in him is ignited. Not consciously, so that he desires this and does that; but by seeing and pausing, by praising and imploring in the surroundings of Mary, the mystery of a Christian life is roused and awakened. It is called forth, it breathes, it grows, and it expands.

Chapter 6
Practical Considerations

And now we must say a few words about the different ways of praying the Rosary, for it has a simple form but its substance is wide and deep. This combination makes praying it easy and difficult at the same time: easy for a person with a vivid imagination and an open heart, capable of arresting the picture with the flow of words and identifying his own existence in the holy figures; difficult for him who has bartered his inner contemplative faculties for the multiformity of modern life.

So if a person belonging to the second order wishes to pray the Rosary, he must be prepared to grapple with some difficulty. He must practice, and learn gradually what comes naturally to others. Above all, he has to subdue his repugnance to repetition, for this is an essential part of the Rosary. The quiet rhythm of the same words is its form.

He must also subdue the restlessness so deeply entrenched in modern man. One who cannot do this had better not give a thought to the Rosary. He will not only be disappointed, but will run the danger of attaching little value to something beautiful. The Rosary is a prayer of lingering. One must take one's time for it, putting the necessary time at its disposal, not only externally but internally. One who wants to pray it rightly must put away those things that press upon him and become for a time purposeless and quiet. This is necessary, whether he has thirty or ten minutes at his disposal. Neither should he attempt too much. It is not necessary to ramble through the whole Rosary; it is better to say only one or two decades, and to say them right.

Into this one may take his whole life — joys and sorrows, men and things, everything — as he would take it to someone whose presence he finds restful, not to find out how he might act with more success, but to put everything into a proper light. The real meditation takes place in the Hail Mary.

The first part of the prayer consists in beholding and penetrating, in understanding and praising whatever mystery it is that follows the name of Jesus. After that, one's thoughts are suspended for a while in contemplation. In the second part of the prayer one turns to Mary as the center of the mystery, asking her intercession "now and at the hour of our death." All petitions for body and soul, one's own and those of others, personal and general, are laid before her, and above all, the petition to participate in the mystery of Christ.

In reading these directions for the first time, one may receive the impression that they are complicated and difficult. This impression may grow even stronger if one tries to carry them out, and one may possibly become discouraged and provoked. The point is to realize that one has something to learn. This is a paramount truth, and the crux is the linking together of one's heart's desires and one's conception of the mystery with the words of the prayer.

The following illustration may serve to make this relationship clearer. When I speak to a person, it may be that I have something definite to tell him. In that case, my attention is concentrated on using the right words and on making my hearer understand them properly. My attention runs, so to speak, along a single track. But it may also be that we have a quiet conversation, and that the words do not run along a prescribed course but wander here and there. I then speak to my listener and watch whether he grasps what I mean. I follow closely his bearing and gestures, sense his motives, and feel his whole reaction. I observe the surroundings; pictures of other people enter; events of the past emerge, and the future steps forward. This means that my attention is spread out. It does not have the shape of a line but resembles instead a space. It acts, one might say, symphonically; it sees the background in the foreground, the essence in the gesture, and the past and the future in the present.

One might say the same about the action in the Rosary. It is not directed toward anything definite; it is all-embracing. It is not sharp-cut, but unconstrained. The words are not anchored to a special meaning but left free, so that pictures that are not directly related to them may also emerge. The person praying not only looks at these pictures but dwells in their company, feels them, speaks to them, and allows his own life to pour into them. In this way a quietly moving world comes into being, a world in which the prayer moves with a freedom that is bound only by the number of repetitions and the theme of the mystery.

This has to be learned, of course, and it requires patience. A loving patience, one is tempted to say: the kind of patience a person needs when he strives for something beautiful and alive, and does not give in until it reveals itself.

Although the Our Father before each decade must not be prayed like the Hail Mary, each of the words in it should retain its own meaning. It is the "Lord's Prayer"; we must shield it carefully; and yet, in the sequence of the Rosary it will always have a ring of its own.

The start and the goal of all spiritual movement is the Father. So the prayer to Him is placed at the beginning of each decade, to ask Him for the things that are really vital. The meditation that follows is thus made in the sight of the Father; like the seer in the Revelation of St. John we look at all the different events that pass before the eyes of Him "who sits on the throne, who lives forever and ever."[18]

The Creed is the introduction to the whole Rosary. In it, the Faith is expressed in its entirety. And, finally, with the "Glory be to the Father, and to the Son, and to the Holy Spirit" at the end of each decade, he who prays bows before the triune God, from whom everything comes and to whom everything returns.

[18] Rev. 4:9.

Part 2

A Short Interpretation
of the Mysteries of the Rosary

It has been pointed out before that each decade of the Rosary contains a *mystery*, an event in the life of Jesus, as its special subject for meditation. This mystery is named in the short sentence that follows the name of Jesus in the Hail Mary.

There are fifteen such mysteries, divided into three cycles named in accordance with their character: the Joyful, the Sorrowful, and the Glorious Rosary. The first one contains the events of Jesus' childhood, the second those of His Passion and death, and the third those of His glorification. In this way they span His whole life, and, united with His own, the life of Mary.

The deeper we penetrate into these mysteries, the plainer we see that they contain the basic laws, as it were, of Christian growth — the sacred birth of which we spoke.

In what follows we attempt a short interpretation of the Rosary mysteries. We cannot do better than give a few hints, and even those only within the limits of the author's perception of these holy truths. And here we do not set up any rules. On the contrary, the more the meditation is based on the resources of the person praying, the better and more alive it is.

Since events from Holy Scripture are involved, one might do well to open and read the New Testament, and see what is said there about the message of the angel, Mary's visit to Elizabeth, the birth of the divine Child, and so on. He who prays his Rosary frequently runs the danger of dwelling always on the same pictures and thus his ideas become impoverished. The prayer is much more alive if he takes only one or two decades instead of the whole Rosary, and after reading the sacred texts, allows their richness and vigor to act upon him. The different words and details are taken from the Gospels and the Acts, and I would like to suggest the use of a so-called "Gospel harmony" book, in which the biblical events are united in an uninterrupted narrative. Perhaps the author's own book *The Lord*[19] might also be of good service.

---

[19] Romano Guardini, *The Lord* (Chicago: Henry Regnery Co., 1954).

Chapter 1

The Prologue of Each Rosary

Each cycle of five decades is preceded by a prelude, in which the person praying makes his preparation. It consists of the Creed, the Our Father, and three Hail Marys, of which each also contains a sort of mystery in the form of a petition for those primary forces of Christian life that are known in the Church as the evangelical virtues.

St. Paul speaks of them in his first letter to the Corinthians, in which he contrasts these virtues with the extraordinary workings of the Holy Spirit and shows their essential importance: "So there abide faith, hope, and charity, these three; but the greatest of these is charity."[20]

In these virtues the greatest forces of the human spirit and heart make themselves manifest. But they are rooted in God; they are ways and directions for the operation of God's living perfection in man. In them

[20] 1 Cor. 13:13.

His holy truth becomes faith, His consummated will becomes hope; but as for charity, which is given precedence by Paul, our human heart gives with its love the answer to Him who "has loved us first!"[21]

---

[21] 1 John 4:10.

Faith

". . . Jesus, Whom we ask to increase our faith."

When Mary crossed the mountains to visit Elizabeth and to find someone with whom she might speak, the latter, filled with the Holy Spirit, received her young relative with words of love and devotion: "Blessed is she who has believed, because the things promised her by the Lord shall be accomplished."[22]

The uniqueness of Mary easily leads to the opinion that her life was filled with miracles and visions; but this opinion would obliterate the foremost truth of her life. Elizabeth's word re-establishes Mary, praising her for her faith. That was her greatness: that she believed, and remained believing to the end of her life. But is faith really something so great if one experiences what she

[22] Luke 1:45.

experienced? It must be so, because the evangelist has a purpose when he tells us how the same angel who visited Mary also came to Zachary to bring him God's promise. Zachary knew it was God's messenger who spoke to him; still, he did not accept the message, and the angel punished him, "because thou hast not believed my words."[23]

Mary had faith. She bowed before God as the Lord of creation, certain that He could make His word come true beyond all natural possibilities. She entered on the unknown road along which He called her. This road led ever further into the mystery, and only her faith gave her the strength to follow the road to the end. The sentence "And they did not understand the word that He spoke to them,"[24] stands for Mary's whole life. She "understood" only in the abundance and grace of Pentecost; earlier she was forced to trust and to obey.

Faith is the foundation of our Christian life. It is awakened by God's Revelation. In fact, it has grown out of that very root, for the same power in which God makes Himself known to us, also enables us to hear His

[23] Luke 1:20.
[24] Luke 2:50.

word and remain faithful to Him. With this the new life starts; not with one's own reason and strength, but with God's word and grace. As soon as faith diminishes, we are like Peter on the sea — we sink. We always need faith, and the more the longer we live. The more life broadens, the more faith we need, because we learn more of how impenetrable human existence is. So we ask the Lord that He may "increase our faith."

Hope

". . . Whom we ask to strengthen our hope."

Elizabeth calls the Virgin blessed because she had faith, for everything would happen as the Lord had told her: through the Holy Spirit she would become the mother of the Redeemer and in this way find the fulfillment of her life and salvation. To be assured of this was not always easy. When the Gospel speaks of Mary and her Son, one perceives a great love, but also a certain remoteness. The answer of the twelve-year-old boy in the Temple;[25] the answer Jesus gave to Mary at the wedding feast of Cana;[26] His words to the bystanders, when Mary, at the door, asks for Him;[27] what He said to the woman

[25] Luke 2:49.
[26] John 2:4.
[27] Mark 3:33.

who exalted His mother;[28] and His last testament in which He committed her to the care of the disciple[29] — in each of these, something is revealed that removes Him from her, and we always sense the possibility that she might have become perplexed about God's guidance.

But each time her confidence increased and she placed everything into His hands. Mary lived completely through her confidence in God's power, a power that is capable of bringing all things to perfection, even in darkness and opposition.

Hope is confidence in God's power to accomplish all things. He has promised that we shall become new men, and that His creation shall be a "new Heaven and a new earth."[30]

This is challenged by the impression made on us by worldly things; by the course our life is taking; by the opinions of people around us; by our own daily insufficiency and sin — in short, by everything.

Hope is the "nevertheless" of faith. In spite of every contradiction, the new life is within us, and God will

[28] Luke 11:28.
[29] John 19:26.
[30] Rev. 21:1.

bring it to completion if we trust in Him despite all opposition. But that is difficult, sometimes even impossible. And so we must ask again that the Lord "may strengthen our hope."

Charity

". . . Whom we ask to enkindle our charity."

When Holy Scripture speaks of love, we must never forget that this is the language of Revelation. It speaks not only figuratively of something familiar and substantial, but tells us something that we do not know from our own experience. The love of which it speaks has its source in God. The Apostle expresses it precisely: "In this is love, not that we have loved God, but that He has first loved us, and sent His Son to be a propitiation for our sins."[31]

These words sound so familiar that we easily miss the grandeur that is hidden in them. We might infer that God means well toward us; but the fact that He loves us

---

[31] 1 John 4:10.

so greatly that He sacrificed His Son for us is in itself Revelation pure and simple. God is driven by His great love to give Himself to us, not out of some dark impulse, but in the unblemished freedom of His eternal sovereignty: "For God so loved the world that He gave His only-begotten Son, that those who believe in Him may not perish, but may have life everlasting."[32]

The angel's message to Mary was the request that she receive this love in her heart, and henceforth live out of it. It is here that Christian love began on earth. The answer Mary gave to the message was a surpassing of herself, a readiness to obey. Out of this grew not only her felicity — remember the jubilant praises that mounted from her heart when she greeted Elizabeth[33] — but also her lasting sacrifice.

Over and over again, Mary had to re-enact what seemed to be God's self-abandonment in Him who was her one and all. Again and again, her Son was taken from her into alien parts, in obedience to the will of the Father, until at the last hour, when she would no longer be His mother only, He said to her, "Woman, behold thy

[32] John 3:16.
[33] Luke 1:46-55.

son."[34] To accept this, to stand the test over and over, and to grow ever more in charity, was the meaning of her whole life.

When we hear of the love of God, we understand it instinctively out of our own human love, as its completion and sanctification. In truth, it is the consummation of the love that is of God. It means that beyond ourselves we merge into His love, and that this love begins with obedience: "For this is the love of God, that we keep His commandments."[35] And obedience it remains, only now the obedience that was burdensome in the beginning has become joyful and free. Out of this comes the essential meaning of our life: that in it the will of God matters more than our own. We may surmise the meaning of this when we read the words from the letter to the Romans: "For I am sure that neither death, nor life, nor angels, nor principalities, nor things present, nor things to come, nor powers, nor height, nor depth, nor any other creature will be able to separate us from the love of God, which is in Jesus Christ our Lord."[36]

[34] John 19:26.
[35] 1 John 5:3.
[36] Rom. 8:38-39.

Chapter 2

The Joyful Rosary

The Annunciation

". . . Whom thou, O Virgin,
didst conceive of the Holy Spirit."

This mystery speaks of that most truly peaceful hour in which the fate of the world was reversed. It speaks of the longing of a creation lost in sin and remoteness from God; of the unfathomable decree of the Eternal Father to embrace it in a new effusion of grace; of the first approach of the Son toward us.

This first joyful mystery speaks of the angel's message to Mary, which is at the same time a summons and a question: "Behold, thou shalt conceive in thy womb and shalt bring forth a son; and thou shalt call His name Jesus."[37]

[37] Luke 1:31.

And it speaks of the unconditional readiness of the purest of all women to be the one from whom the Son of God accepted our human form: "Behold the hand-maid of the Lord; be it done to me according to thy word."[38] No event was ever surrounded by greater tranquillity. No deed was ever done more simply. But the decision that was made there reached from earth to Heaven.

The event is re-enacted, spiritually, in the life of every one of the faithful. Above all, it is re-enacted when man is touched for the first time by the person and the word of Christ — be it through another man, a book, or an inner experience — and he recognizes the truth and craves to embrace it. The Lord, in His body and living might, enters into him at this moment. Now begins, as we mentioned before, the penetration and growth of Christ in man; the reshaping of man in Him. From here on, the summons is always repeated. Every hearing of Christ's truth, every radiation of His image, every reminder of His commandments demands that we take Him deep into our hearts and put ourselves at His disposal willingly.

[38] Luke 1:31, 38.

The Visitation

". . . Whom thou, O Virgin,
didst bear with thee to Elizabeth."

This is the time after the angel's Annunciation that was, for Mary, at once happy and distressing. No woman has ever borne such gladness within her. But neither was any woman ever imprisoned in such silence. For how could she speak of the event so that the listener would believe her? Not even he to whom she was espoused for life understood until an angel enlightened him in a dream.[39]

Here began the serious part of resignation. For honor or dishonor, for life and death, she was in God's hands. She left her home, and crossed the mountains to Elizabeth, that motherly woman to whom she was connected

[39] Matt. 1:20.

by old ties of trust. She, who was often afflicted, would know what had happened. And she did know, for the spirit that had worked the mystery in Mary also filled Elizabeth, so that she knew the truth before Mary said a word: "Blessed art thou among women and blessed is the fruit of thy womb!"[40] The whole mystery is filled with the unspeakable intimacy in which Mary carried the life of the God-Man, giving Him hers and receiving of His.

In every Christian life there is a sacred domain of nascent growth in which dwells Christ — a domain in which we are more firmly rooted than we are in our own. There He works and grows, takes possession of our being, draws our strength toward Himself, penetrates our thoughts and volition, and sways our emotions and sentiments, so that the word of the Apostle comes true: "It is now no longer I that live, but Christ lives in me."[41]

[40] Luke 1:42.
[41] Gal. 2:20.

The Nativity

". . . Who was born to thee, O Virgin."

It is the hour of the Holy Night. The divine Child Jesus comes forth into the outer world, becomes our brother, and takes upon Himself the lot of the Redeemer. "And it came to pass while they were there, that the days for her to be delivered were fulfilled. And she brought forth her firstborn son."[42] These words are addressed to us all, and the glorification of that joyous happening will never be muted on this earth.

At the same hour something happened that concerned Mary alone: in her own personal being, in her spirit and heart, Christ moved into the open expanse of her perception and love; the attitude of expectation

[42] Luke 2:6-7.

became a communion face-to-face. Unutterable truth — she saw Him who was the manifestation of the living God! As her heart overflowed, a flaming flood rushed toward Him who came with the love of the Redeemer. Serving Him in His tender years, she served the Lord who had revealed Himself in human weakness.

This takes place spiritually in every Christian as often as that inner life which is divined by faith steps into the clarity of knowledge, into the distinctness of action, and into the decisiveness of testimony. In every one of us Christ is born as often as He penetrates, as essence and standard, into any deed or happening. One day this happens with particular significance: namely, on that day when it dawns on us, clear and strong, who Christ is, so that He becomes the governing reality of our inner lives.

The Presentation

". . . Whom thou, O Virgin, didst offer in the Temple."

This mystery is concerned with the journey Mary took, forty days after her confinement, to the Temple of God in Jerusalem to offer her Child to Him in accordance with the Jewish Law.

Every first-begotten child belonged to God, but this one in a manner that went beyond expression. Full of quiet dignity in her poverty, Mary placed the Child in the arms of the priest who gave Him back to her after a small offering.

Simeon revealed to those who heard him the fate of the Redeemer, and to Mary the tribulations to be inflicted on the mother: "Behold, this Child is destined for the fall and for the rise of many in Israel, and for a sign that shall be contradicted. And thy own soul a sword shall pierce, that the thoughts of many hearts may be revealed."[43]

In the sweetness of this first friendly gathering there rings a bitter note of suffering. Mary has received her Child from God and put her whole being at His disposal. He was her one and all; but He was not her own. The first festive act of her motherhood was a sacrifice.

What God has given us, if we believe and obey, does not belong to us by nature. The new life is not ours like a talent or a characteristic; it is a gift, and it remains a gift. It is governed by God's will and guidance, and we must always be ready for a call away from ourselves, a transfer to duty, renunciation, and destiny that have their meaning only in the will of God.

[43] Luke 2:34-35.

The Finding of the
Child Jesus in the Temple

". . . Whom thou, O Virgin, didst find in the Temple."

Twelve years lie between this event and the one before, and eighteen will pass before the next. Those years are surrounded by the silence that covers the childhood, youth, and young manhood of Christ in Holy Scripture. Apart from what the Gospels tell us of this first period, we hear nothing for over thirty years.

One single event comes forth: Jesus, when He was twelve years old, complied with the Law and made His first pilgrimage to Jerusalem. There He remained in the Temple without the knowledge of His parents; and Mary passed through a torment of anxiety over her Child.

When she finally found Him again, "sitting in the midst of the teachers, listening to them and asking them questions," she might have felt an even greater anguish, for to her sad question, "Son, why hast thou done so to us?" she received the answer, "How is it that you sought me? Did you not know that I must be about my Father's business?"[44]

A terrible blow struck deep into her maternal heart and took her Child away: the will of the Father. How hard this was and how great the strangeness was that touched her heart is shown in the next sentence: "And they did not understand the word that He spoke to them."[45] Yet the joy of finding Him again was a sustaining reward.

All of this repeats itself spiritually in the life of every believer. At first, Christ is the center; our faith in Him is firm and loving. But then He disappears for a while, often suddenly and apparently without the slightest reason.

A remoteness has been created. A void is formed. We feel forsaken. Faith seems folly. "Against all hope," we must maintain hope. Everything becomes heavy, wearisome, and senseless. We must walk alone and seek.

[44] Luke 2:49.
[45] Luke 2:50.

But one day we find Christ again — and it is in such circumstances that the power of the Father's will becomes evident to us.

Chapter 3

The Sorrowful Rosary

graveness with which God views our salvation, a graveness so profound that He not only gave this salvation, but Himself assumed human nature and became the Child of this mother.

This graveness breaks through forcefully in the mysteries of the second Rosary. They also reveal God's love, but do so by showing us the frightfulness of sin. Indeed because sin blinds us, we cannot even answer for ourselves the question of what sin really is. Its meaning dawns upon us when we realize what God has done to triumph over it. It is that frightful thing which God in His omniscience and justice decreed must be expiated through the suffering and death of the Incarnate Word.

The Agony in the Garden

". . . Who sweat blood for us."

The hour of Gethsemane is inexhaustible. We all must draw from it as much as our hearts can hold.

Let us stress the words "He began to feel dread and to be exceedingly troubled,"[47] and "His sweat became as drops of blood running down upon the ground."[48] It is the horror of the Redeemer before sin, not only before the Passion and death as such, but before the fact that all this must be endured in expiation for our sins, and that He was meant to take them upon Himself and be responsible for them. How terrible it must have been is shown by the other words He speaks in prayer: "Father,

[47] Mark 14:33.
[48] Luke 22:44.

all things are possible to Thee. Remove this cup from me."[49] What was to come went against the Redeemer's whole being; not only because death is a revolt against the will to live, but because sin is a revolt against God. His third exclamation is "Yet not what I will, but what Thou willest."[50]

The worst part of sin is its hiddenness. It hides everywhere: under the pretense that it is something natural, that it is something unavoidable, and that the power, gravity, or tragedy of life is expressed by it. If we are witnesses here of Christ's fate, our eyes are opened wide to this pretense.

It is an important moment in the life of a Christian when he is touched for the first time by horror at the reality of sin. On every side we meet this horror — but the creature does not know what it is that frightens him most deeply.

All existence labors beneath the spell of sin. In Christ's anguish it breaks through to a last and most terrible transparency. Because of it, the Son of God feels the terror of this hour. But each of us must himself

[49] Mark 14:36.
[50] Ibid.

realize, in the deepest part of his being, that what is revealed here is the fearfulness of his own sins.

The next three mysteries deal with the agony the Lord had to suffer before His death. Between them lies what the Gospel tells us of the arrest, the trial, and the condemnation of Christ. It is difficult to say anything about these mysteries. They deal with the wretchedness of humanity, and of the way the Lord accepted and bore this wretchedness. Their content is endless. We can extract only one point at a time, and he who prays must see how he progresses.

The Scourging of Our Lord

". . . Who was scourged for us."

"Pilate, then, took Jesus and had Him scourged."[51]

To beat a person is an act of frightful distinctness: the original beginning of hatred against the feeling and breathing life-force of him who is hated. Sin, as hatred against God, strikes the Redeemer with these blows. It desires to cause Him suffering. His whole body must become a vessel of pain. His holy vitality must be destroyed. And it is a special sin that attacks Him here: the sin of the senses. Its cupidity is transformed into suffering for the Lord.

Christianity does not say that the body is evil and its passion sin — not that sin cannot enter passion, or evil

---

[51] John 19:1.

find root in the body. To become a Christian does not mean to despise or destroy the body, but to do away with blindness and to recognize the evil that is at work in nature. It means to fight for purity of body and soul, and even to accept bodily pain as a means of purification. If the believer does this, it is Christ's purity that penetrates into him.

The Crowning with Thorns

". . . Who was crowned with thorns for us."

"And plaiting a crown of thorns, they put it upon His head. . . . And bending the knee before Him, they mocked Him, saying: Hail, king of the Jews."[52]

The dignity of a man is revealed by his head. The crown is the emblem of the royal majesty which belongs to God.

The mockery here is directed against the head of the Lord, who wears invisibly the crown of the "King of Kings." The soldiers make a "mock king" out of Him. But behind their hollow cruelty lies another wish, one that seeks to make of Him — we venture the word — a "mock god." All the mockery on earth is combined here

---

[52] Matt. 27:29.

to abolish God's dignity, and with it the dignity of man which is rooted in God.

Man's life is interwoven with pride, rebellion, and vanity — sometimes open, mostly hidden. Their roots are invisible to human eyes and they stretch beyond the human will. The Lord unveils their power by giving them the possibility of being turned against Himself. The pride with which we strut about and the vanities we relish are transformed for the Son of God into a pattern of humiliation. His suffering is as great as the measure of human evil.

It is a decisive moment in the growth of a Christian when he penetrates the deceit of all that is called greatness: power, accomplishment, beauty, reputation. Of course, these things are not evil in themselves, but evil is in them. Now is the time to meditate on all of this, to hold firmly one's ground, and to acquire self-knowledge. And then one should fight for humility.

Humility is nothing other than the conviction that God is God, and only God — and that man is man, and nothing but man.

The Carrying of the Cross

". . . Who carried the heavy Cross for us."

The Gospel says, "And bearing the Cross for Himself, Jesus went forth to the place that is called the Skull (in Hebrew, *Golgotha*)."[53] How full of meaning are these words, which imply the carrying of a burden that goes beyond His strength. Finally they meet a "certain Simon of Cyrene, coming from the country, and upon him they laid the Cross to bear it after Jesus," because He could not go on.[54] Everything that means a burden in life is shown here in its last fearfulness: toil, destitution, pain, the people around one, one's own existence, a heavy heart, the inner void, the unbearableness of all things.

[53] John 19:17.
[54] Luke 23:26.

In the last analysis, everything is a "burden," not because it is painful instead of joyous, but because sin has stamped it with the curse of hardship. Man seeks to escape it. He will not take it upon his shoulders and persevere beneath it. Indolence, cowardice, resistance against the hardships of life, all mean here for Christ the obligation to carry a weight that is beyond His strength.

The old doctrine of the spiritual life calls indolence the first and most stubborn infirmity of man. We can see here what this means. We can also be enlightened about ourselves: about the condition of our lives, about the loads we carry, the hardships we endure, the tasks in which we must persevere — about our own life's burdens, and those embodied in human existence.

The last sorrowful mystery once more summarizes everything. Like the first, it too is inexhaustible. We must approach it with open eyes and heart, examine what takes place, and persevere — conscious that all this concerns our very own selves.

The Crucifixion

". . . Who was crucified for us."

Before the end, the Lord spoke the words "It is consummated."[55] The whole fifth mystery speaks of this; all "is consummated." What happened here had its prelude in the creation of the world, the time when all things were generated. Then sin tore everything asunder, and all was lost. Now the Lord draws everything back again unto His bosom, and suffers it in a way that is known only to Himself. In this He reaches into the abyss of grace and lets it gush forth. And from this issues the new creation. The new start that is given to us, the forces from which the "new man"[56] in us can grow and rise into eternity,

[55] John 19:30.
[56] Eph. 4:24.

the new Heaven and the new earth that will one day surround us[57] — all of these issue from this hour.

And we must know this. We become Christians in the measure that we are awakened and penetrated by this knowledge of the agony and death which Christ suffered. From this point onwards our own suffering is transformed.

While our suffering was formerly only the consequence of our guilt, it is now part of the mystery of the Cross. It shares in the force that changes the old existence into the new. In the eyes of the world, suffering is inconsolable to the last. Nothing can really help it. Mostly we do not notice it, because it does not last very long, or because our attention is diverted. But when it becomes great and we have to face it, then we see there is only one help for our suffering, and that help comes from suffering itself.

Since the time of Christ's Passion it has always been so. It was then that there was raised up a fearful and blessed ground onto which we might safely step; and the strength was given us to change the old life into the new if we suffer together with Christ. If man understands this

[57] Rev. 21:1.

mystery and commits himself to it, he has reached the center of all things, and all goes well.

But where in all this does Mary remain? We have not spoken of her because Scripture, in its account of the last days of Jesus, does not do so. She is mentioned only at the end, when we are told that "now there was standing by the Cross of Jesus His mother."[58] This sentence covers all the preceding events. She always stood "beneath the Cross," and never withdrew from the holy and terrible domain of Christ's Passion. It was natural for her to be present in whatever place it happened. And it was just as natural that she would come to know all that had occurred.

Every breath the Lord drew passed through Mary's breast; every throb of His heart was her own; and nothing happened to Him that had not also "penetrated her soul," as Simeon had foretold. So we must draw her into all of these events.

Mary connects us with all these happenings. It is she who causes us not only to look and meditate, but also makes us aware that all these happenings concern every one of us, you and me. She is the reason that I do not

[58] John 19:25.

run away when my faintheartedness becomes unbearable, but that I remain. She herself remained, "until all was consummated."[59]

And so must I.

<hr />

[59] Cf. Matt. 5:18; Mark 13:30; Luke 21:32.

Chapter 4

The Glorious Rosary

The third cycle is the Glorious Rosary. It speaks of the completion of these sacred happenings. It tells us of those things that seemed to be defeat and failure, but which were in fact a victory. These things were not a victory in a human sense, although even humanly speaking, the victor is not the person who silences the testimony of truth, but rather the one who maintains it to the end, for in some way it will prevail.

But here we are not concerned with anything of this kind. We are concerned with God, who has created the world, who has surrounded it with His love, who has become man, and who has suffered the guilt and doom of the world.

Through all of this, something in the world was changed, once and for all. A new creation emerged. It stands; no power can extinguish it; and any man of good will may share in the holy beginning. This last cycle of the Rosary speaks of the splendor that rose behind the darkness of Jesus' death.

The second cycle comprises the events of those last days between the eve of Holy Thursday and the night of Easter. What happened prior to this is not told in detail, but is part of the last set of mysteries. We do not hear that Jesus left His home and appeared publicly; that He preached, taught, and fought; that He had no contact with men and endured untold solitude; that the Kingdom of God did not arrive as it might have arrived had "His own received Him";[46] that hatred had closed in around Him, and that that which for almost fifteen hundred years had resisted God now gathered for a last onslaught.

The mysteries of the Joyful Rosary, taken separately, might easily slide into the idyllic or sentimental, if the sad note of its fourth mystery did not act as a warning. In fact, they are a revelation, not of the loveliness and closeness that lie between mother and child, but of the

---

[46] John 1:11.

The First
Glorious Mystery

The Resurrection

". . . Who arose from the dead."

The death of our Lord is wrapped in mystery. He suffered a death more grievous than man can suffer because He was more truly alive than any man. And yet, when the Lord spoke of His death, He also spoke of His Resurrection. "From that time Jesus began to show His disciples that He must go to Jerusalem and suffer many things from the elders and scribes and chief priests, and be put to death, and on the third day rise again."[60]

The disciples did not understand His words; their whole manner at His death shows this. But she who must have known the truth was Mary. She had given Him His human life, His breath and growth. His every

[60] Matt. 16:21.

movement had taken place before her eyes and heart for thirty years. She had stood beneath the Cross and she had seen Him die; so she knew that His life was of a special kind. When the women and Peter and John spoke to her of the empty tomb and the words of the angel, it must all have been just as she had expected it to be. And she whose heart had been placed in the tomb with the body of her Son, arose with Him in the light of His divine victory.

Paul says in the letter to the Romans that "our old self" should be "crucified" and die and be "buried in Christ."[61] If this happens, then "as Christ has arisen from the dead through the glory of the Father, so we also may walk in newness of life."[62]

This dying and entombing of the old self is a constant process within us through every struggle against evil, through every conquest of self, through every suffering which is bravely borne, through every sacrifice of love and charity. But through this dying of the old self, the resurrection of the new man is also accomplished. At times, very deep within us, and covered by earthly

[61] Rom. 6:6, 4.
[62] Rom. 6:4.

insufficiency and calamities, we feel the secret spark of this ever holy and living flame, which is the "glory of the sons of God."[63] For the rest, we have to believe.

[63] Rom. 8:21.

The Ascension

". . . Who ascended into Heaven."

After His Resurrection, the Lord remained with His friends those forty days of which the Gospels speak. From the same Mount of Olives that witnessed the beginning of His Passion, "He was lifted up before their eyes"[64] and disappeared into Heaven.

Mary may not have been with them when this happened. From all reports, only those were present who had been there before. We do not know if the Lord told her exactly when He would "go to the Father."[65] But there was a tender companionship between Him and His mother which did not need explicit wording, so that

[64] Acts 1:9.
[65] John 14:12.

she would know what was to happen. Then she was alone. It applied to her, above all, when Paul said, "If you have risen with Christ, seek the things that are above, where Christ is seated at the right hand of God. Mind the things that are above, not the things that are on earth."[66] Her Son was "above," and her heart was with Him, and her whole being strove upward to Him.

When the Lord lifted Himself from the earth, there began the wait "until He comes."[67] Ever since Christ's Ascension, on earth there has been a single confident expectation; and faith means to persevere in this expectation. For him who has no faith, events take place as though their meaning lay in themselves. The ordinary and the exceptional, the high and the low, the frightful and the beautiful — everything that makes history — all are regarded as if each was by itself and there were nothing besides. In truth, the Lord's departure was like the striking of a mighty chord that is now suspended in the air waiting to float away and come to rest. But only with Christ's return will all things be fulfilled.

[66] Col. 3:1-2.
[67] 1 Cor. 11:26.

The Descent
of the Holy Spirit

". . . Who hath sent us the Holy Spirit."

The night before His Passion, the Lord had said to His disciples, "I will not leave you orphans."[68] When He had gone, they really became orphans, for God was now no longer present with them in the manner in which He had been present through Christ. But on the day of Pentecost, God returned in the Holy Spirit, who was sent by Him. Now the disciples' orphanhood was ended; the friend, the "Advocate,"[69] the heavenly guide, was with them. But His task was to teach them the whole truth, and to give them Christ.

[68] John 14:18.
[69] John 14:16.

Mary was also among those upon whom the Holy Spirit descended. The Gospel specifically says this, and we may perhaps surmise a little of what the gift, accompanied by the roar of the divine wind and the flames, must have meant to her. As often as the Gospel speaks of her, we may sense some slight remoteness between the human mother and the mystery of her divine Son. The sentence "And they did not understand the word that He spoke to them,"[70] may serve as an illustration. And now with the coming of the Holy Spirit all is perfectly clear. No perplexities could remain, and every event had its meaning.

The Holy Spirit is also sent to us. Through His coming we are no longer orphans. He is with us, if only we ourselves will stay with Him. He leads our lives through all that is concealed, but we must leave our hand in His. If we beseech Him and open ourselves up to Him with heart and soul, He shows us how to know Christ, and in Christ ourselves. But where darkness prevails because our earthly life is shut off from Christ, He gives us a divine "nevertheless" — as Paul says, a "testimony to our spirit that we are sons of God" and the

[70] Luke 2:50.

certainty that "for those who love God all things work together unto good."[71]

The next two glorious mysteries are not taken from Scripture but from Christian Revelation. The source of our faith is the word of God; but we must not forget that the "word of God" is not only the written word, but also the word that was spoken by word of mouth by those who were given the task to "make disciples of all nations . . . even unto the consummation of the world."[72] From this divine source the Church completes the story of Mary's life.

Her life must have been ineffable in its tranquillity; she was present and at the same time withdrawn after the departure of her Son. We do not know how long this life lasted — perhaps a long, long time — for when the Lord died she was barely fifty. How shall we clothe in words the mystery of the time she passed in the keeping of "the disciple whom He loved"?[73] Perhaps we might say she wished nothing more, aspired to nothing, feared nothing, missed nothing, for all had been fulfilled.

[71] Rom. 8:16, 28.
[72] Matt. 28:19-20.
[73] John 19:26.

When the Holy Spirit descended on the disciples, He equipped them for their mighty work. When at the same time He came to Mary, her work was already accomplished. All that remained to do for her was to bring her fuller understanding. From then on she must have lived in ineffable clarity, in indescribable peace. She was waiting, perhaps, for the hour when her Son would call, but in this waiting there was a sense of complete fulfillment. She would have waited a hundred years as well as one day in this peace. From this pure stillness, her words must have fallen like rays of light into the hearts of those who came to her to learn of Jesus; and no one can measure those things that passed from her into the holy message.

The picture of Mary's later life serves us as promise and security. It shows us that we must not take time too seriously, for if we have faith, eternity dwells in us; that we must not overrate the calamities of life, for "the sufferings of the present time are not worthy to be compared with the glory to come that will be revealed in us";[74] and that we must ask God to show us that eternity dwells in the heart of time.

[74] Rom. 8:18.

The Assumption

". . . Who hath assumed thee, O Virgin, into Heaven."

The years of peaceful waiting have come to an end. The Lord has come and called His mother. When her time on earth was over, the Blessed Mother of God was assumed, body and soul united, into the joy and glory of Heaven. The power of His Resurrection was realized in her, and He has taken her into eternity. A mystery of infinite joy! When the Church speaks of it, when lyric poets praise it, when artists portray it, it is as though something breaks through that otherwise would be hidden in the things of this earth. It is not without reason that the feast of Mary's Assumption is observed in the last maturity of summer.

The mystery of the Assumption is given to us so that we may have a foretaste of the meaning of Christian joy, of participation in God's triumph, and of the infinite upsurge of creation. And it is given to us so that a divine ray of light may fall upon our own death.

When the Lord died and rose again, He transformed our dying. Death was the fruit of guilt; no words, no matter how strong, could wipe away this truth. But through Christ's dying, death lost its sting and changed into something else.[75] Dying is no longer something that happens to us as if we were alone, as if it were the termination of our lives in darkness. Rather it is something which comes to us from Christ. Dying now means that Christ comes and calls. Our life is shattered, but through this a door opens; and on the other side stands Christ.

[75] 1 Cor. 15:55.

The Coronation
of the Blessed Virgin in Heaven

". . . Who hath crowned thee, O Virgin, in Heaven."

This mystery completes the one that precedes it. That mystery spoke of Mary's Assumption into eternity, and this one praises the bestowal on her of gifts from the inexhaustible treasury of Heaven. St. Paul said that "those who receive the abundance of grace and the gift of justice reign in [eternal] life through the one Jesus Christ."[76] So a share of Christ's sovereignty is given to her who walked with Him along the dark paths of earth. The crown is the symbol of this. Now she is the "Queen of Heaven." Mary is God's creature — as we are — and submissive to Him in a humility as great as her purity.

[76] Rom. 5:17.

Nevertheless, she is raised to a holy authority that is without pretense or self-will, but is the bestower of generous graces.

The innermost mark of a Christian should be humility. He knows that he has nothing of himself, but that everything comes from God, and that he is unable to do anything without divine grace. The virtue of humility is the acknowledgment of this truth. Yes, it is also the joy in this acknowledgment and the happiness that comes from it — it is, lastly, nothing but love.

Yet in this same humility is buried a peaceful consciousness of hidden kingliness. This kingliness is not our own, but one bestowed on us, and bestowed on us in such a way that it is more deeply our own than any we might claim for ourselves. That is what Paul means when he speaks of "the glory to come that will be revealed in us."[77] It is the supreme splendor of God that shines forth in the risen Christ.

And, as this final mystery of the Rosary promises, we shall have our part in it.

[77] Rom. 8:18.

Appendix
A Suggestion

We have followed the mysteries contained in the Rosary's commonly accepted form. Josef Weiger, in his beautiful book *Maria, Mutter des neuen und ewigen Bundes*, speaks of the importance of the mother of Jesus both in herself and in the history of salvation. Toward the end of this book he also mentions the Rosary, and develops a thought that we may wish to make our own.

When we meditate on the three cycles of the Rosary prayer, we may look for a clearer projection of a truth that governs our present life: namely, the waiting for Christ's return, as shown in the previous mysteries of the third cycle. Weiger proposes substituting for the two mysteries "Who took you, O Virgin, into Heaven," and "Who crowned you, O Virgin, in Heaven," the following: "Who will return to us in glory," and "Whose Kingdom will have no end."

Let us meditate, then, on these two new mysteries and leave it to the reader to make what use of them he sees fit.

The Second Coming of Christ

". . . Who will return to us in glory."

It was revealed to us: "When the Son of Man shall come in His majesty . . . then He will sit on the throne of His glory; and before Him will be gathered all the nations."[78]

The first years of Christian history were filled with the expectation of this coming. Later it was lost. But the message of Christ's return remains indelibly inscribed in the testimonies of faith, and its affirmation lies in the depth of the Christian heart. Christ will return one day; no one knows when. But it will not be, as before, in weakness; as a slave in bondage who waited for the acceptance of his message,[79] but as the Lord in His glory.

[78] Matt. 25:31-32.
[79] Cf. Rom. 8:15, 21.

Then He will put an end to all matter that is temporal. He will extinguish the world within whose frame and history iniquity took root. To mortal men He will issue the call to resurrection and before His omniscient court of justice He will pronounce His verdict and lead men to everlasting life in the measure that they have lived righteously before God.

We live in time, and time is possessed by the delusion of permanence. All things crumble away but are formed anew, so that the world in itself seems imperishable. The living vanish, but out of those things that die, new life is born; so it seems that life, as a whole, continues on its way. The deeds of each man come to an end and his work falls to dust, but these are always started over again. So struggle and strain never cease.

When the Redeemer came and was rebuffed, all seemed veiled and indecipherable. But one day He will return to expose the delusion, and to bring light and fulfillment. Until that day comes, we must be faithful and wait for Him.

Our belief is contradicted on every side. That the Lord will put an end to everything and pronounce His final verdict seems like a children's fairy tale. But to persevere in this belief is "the victory that surmounts the world."[80] This judgment will be terrible, but may it be praised! We are "looking for the blessed hope and glorious coming of our great God and Savior, Jesus Christ."[81] No one can bear up before His judgment, and yet it is the "blessed hope," because in His judgment God's truth will become power and will right all things.

[80] 1 John 5:4.
[81] Titus 2:13.

The Fifth
Glorious Mystery

The Kingdom of God

". . . Whose Kingdom will have no end."

Then the Kingdom of God will come. God's Kingdom will be all and everything, not through external force but through its inner harmony.

So long as time endures here below there is no perfectly triumphant Kingdom of God, for the good man may be overthrown and the evil man may prevail — as happens again and again. Once time has become eternity, truth and reality will be one, as will also power and virtue. But God will be Lord of creation because He is the essence of holiness and justice.

All that contradicted Him will be broken before the judgment seat and cast into a void that no man can describe. Those who have stood the test before the throne, on the other hand, will breathe freely and be happy in God's dominion, for in itself this is freedom and life. "Behold," says the Lord, "I will make all things new." There will be "a new Heaven" and "a new earth," "and they shall see His face and His name shall be on their foreheads"; and "His servants shall serve Him."[82]

For this we wait. While we wait, we know by faith that Christ's kingdom on earth is His Church,[83] leading us to the perfect Kingdom of God in Heaven. The Church is the herald of the Kingdom to come. This Kingdom is already ours, even if only as a promise and a beginning. Insofar as we accept the holy message, insofar as we love God in the midst of coldness and disdain, insofar as we endure the contradiction of all things, we experience a partial fulfillment of the promise.

When God's perfectly triumphant Kingdom does come, we will be not only subjects but co-rulers. That Kingdom will accomplish the liberation of all things in God. And "the glory of the children of God,"[84] wherein we share in His supremacy, is the freedom we will find in Him.

[82] Rev. 21:1, 5; 27:3-4.
[83] Matt. 16:18-19.
[84] Rom. 8:21.

In all this no word has been said of Mary; but she is included. She awaits the hour "the Father has set in His power"[85] when all of this shall come to pass. The Last Judgment of her Son shall vindicate her life before the world. And in His Kingdom her gracious rule shall be resplendent — as we know from the words of the book of Revelation: "A great sign appeared in Heaven: a woman clothed with the sun, and the moon was under her feet, and upon her head a crown of twelve stars."[86]

---

[85] Acts 1:7.
[86] Rev. 12:1.

Biographical Note

Romano Guardini

(1885-1968)

Although he was born in Verona, Italy, Msgr. Romano Guardini grew up in Mainz, Germany, where his father was serving as Italian consul. Since his education and formation were German, he decided to remain in Germany as an adult.

After studying chemistry and economics as a youth, Guardini turned to theology and was ordained to the priesthood in 1910. From 1923 to 1939 (when he was expelled by the Nazis), Msgr. Guardini occupied a chair created for him at the University of Berlin as "professor for the philosophy of religion and Catholic *Weltanschauung*." After the war, similar positions were created for him, first at the University of Tübingen and then at the University of Munich (1948-63). Msgr. Guardini's extremely popular courses in these universities won him a reputation as one of the most remarkable and successful Catholic educators in Germany.

As a teacher, a writer, and a speaker, he was notable for being able to detect and to nurture those elements of spirituality that nourish all that is best in the life of Catholics.

After the war, Msgr. Guardini's influence grew to be enormous, not only through his university positions, but also through the inspiration and guidance he gave to the postwar German Catholic Youth Movement, which enlivened the faith of countless young people.

Msgr. Guardini's writings include works on meditation, education, literature, philosophy, theology, and art. Among his many books, perhaps the most famous is *The Lord,* which has been continuously in print in many languages since its first publication in 1937. Even today, countless readers continue to be transformed by these beautiful books, which combine a profound thirst for God with depth of thought and a delightful perfection of expression.

The works of Msgr. Guardini are indispensable reading for all Christians who want to remain true to the Faith and to grow holy in our age of skepticism and corrosive doubt.

Sophia Institute Press®

Sophia Institute is a nonprofit institution that seeks to restore man's knowledge of eternal truth, including man's knowledge of his own nature, his relation to other persons, and his relation to God.

Sophia Institute Press® serves this end in many ways. It publishes translations of foreign works to make them accessible for the first time to English-speaking readers. It brings back into print books that have been out of print. And it publishes important new books that fulfill the ideals of Sophia Institute. These books afford readers a rich source of the enduring wisdom of mankind.

Sophia Institute Press® makes high-quality books available to the general public by using advanced technology and by soliciting donations to subsidize general publishing costs. Your generosity can help us provide

The Rosary of Our Lady